THE WEAPONS ENCYCLOPÆDIA

TANK AIRCRAFT AFV SHIP ARTILLERY VEHICLES SECRET WEAPON

FIAT C.R. 42 "FALCO"

THE WEAPONS ENCYCLOPAEDIA

PUBLISHED BY

Luca Cristini Editore (Soldiershop), via Orio, 35/4 - 24050 Zanica (BG) ITALY.

DISTRIBUTED BY

Soldiershop - www.soldiershop.com, Amazon, Ingram Spark, Berliner Zinnfigurem (D), LaFeltrinelli, Mondadori, Libera Editorial (Spain), Google book (eBook), Kobo, (eBoook), Apple Book (eBook).

ACKNOWLEDGEMENTS

Special thanks to institutions such as: Stato Maggiore dell'esercito, Archivio di Stato, Bundesarchiv, Nara, Library of Congress ecc. Agli archivi P.Crippa, A.Lopez, L.Manes, C.Cucut, archivi Tallillo. Model Victoria (www.modelvictoria.it). The photos were recoloured by Anna Cristini.

For a complete list of Soldiershop titles, or for every information please contact us on our website: www.soldiershop.com or www. cristinieditore.com. E-mail: info@soldiershop.com. Keep up to date on Facebook & Twitter: https://www.facebook.com/soldiershop. publishing

Title: **FIAT C.R. 42 "FALCO"** Code.: **TWE-009 EN** SERIES by L. S. Cristini
ISBN code: 978-88-93279208. First Edition December 2022

THE WEAPONS ENCYCLOPAEDIA (SOLDIERSHOP) trademark of Luca Cristini Editore

FIAT C.R. 42 "FALCO"

LUCA STEFANO CRISTINI

BOOK SERIES FOR MODELERS & COLLECTORS

CONTENTS

▼ War postcard Fiat C.R.42 "Falco" Regia Aeronautica, 23rd squadron of the 70th Group in Sicily, aircraft of Major Commander Tito Falconi (see profile 6) Licence CC0 1.0 PD.

INTRODUCTION

The Fiat C.R.42 Falco was a famous Italian sesquiplane-type, single-seat, single-engine fighter and night fighter biplane with a fixed undercarriage and mixed (part metal and part canvas) metal structure, made by the famous Turin-based manufacturer in the late 1930s to a design by engineer Celestino Rosatelli. It was used in the Second World War mainly by the Regia Aeronautica, but it was also purchased by countries such as Belgium, Hungary, Finland and Sweden. The 'Falco' (hawk), as the Italian aircraft was nicknamed, was the last biplane fighter in history to be built in series. Together with the British Gloster Gladiator and the Soviet Polikarpov I-15, (to which it was superior) it was also the last biplane fighter to fight in the Second World War and the last biplane in history to shoot down an enemy aircraft in 1945.

The C.R.42 was produced until 1944 and still holds the record for the largest number of Italian aircraft built (around 1,800). The C.R.42 was an evolution of Fiat's earlier C.R.32 fighter (author of major successes in Spain in 1936), with a Fiat A.74R1C.38 air-cooled radial engine. The aircraft immediately proved to be very agile in the air, a factor due to its very low wing loading, which ended up being an often decisive tactical advantage.

RAF intelligence praised its exceptional manoeuvrability, also noting that 'the aircraft was tremendously strong', although it stood little chance against faster and more heavily armed monoplanes. Its best performance came with the Hungarian Air Force on the Eastern Front, where the casualty ratio was 12 to 1. Although used primarily as a fighter, several other roles were adopted for some variants of the type, such as the C.R.42CN night fighter, the C.R.42AS ground attack aircraft and the C.R.42B two-seater trainer.

▼ Diagram of C.R. 42 'Falco'. PD work, released under CC0 1.0 licence.

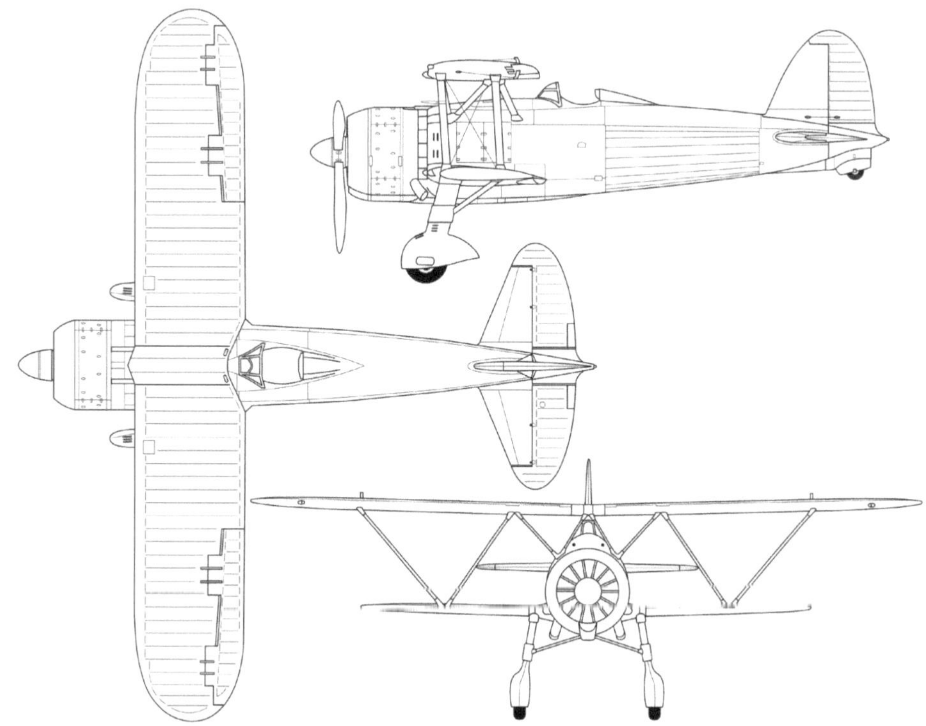

■ DEVELOPMENT AND HISTORY

In 1935-36, building on the great success of its predecessor, especially on Spanish soil during the civil war - the Fiat C.R.32 'Freccia' - the Fiat engineering department headed by engineer Celestino Rosatelli began work on its successor, the Fiat C.R.42 'Falco'. The new biplane was equipped with a Fiat A.74 RC. 38 14-cylinder double-star engine producing 840 hp at 3800 m altitude. Designed by engineers Tranquillo Zerbi and Antonio Fessia, the new engine was a development of the Pratt & Whitney R-1830 SC-4 Twin Wasp.

As already mentioned, that of the biplane fighter was by then an outdated formula and the flight and armament characteristics of FIAT's new fighter were clearly inferior to those of the foreign aircraft that the 'Falco' would face during the Second World War; but the incredible successes that its predecessor C.R.32 was achieving in the Spanish Civil War, even against the much more modern machines fielded by the Soviet Union, such as the Polikarpov, unfortunately convinced the Regia Aeronautica that the formula was still valid, not considering that the results obtained by the C.R.32 were due, yes, to the validity of the machine, but also and above all to the lesser experience and technical value of the enemy aviators.

Moreover, the C.R.32 was designed for combat tactics along the lines of those used during the First World War, techniques that are now unsuitable and outdated.

The result was the creation of a fantastic biplane, the best in history, but unfortunately out of time and destined for combat with much more modern machines.

The Ministry of Aeronautics nevertheless ordered the new biplane on 10 February 1938, issuing a specification for the supply of two intermediate prototypes C.R.40 and C.R.41. Eventually, the first C.R.42 flew over the Turin-Aeritalia airport on 23 May 1938 at the controls of test pilot Valentino Cus.

■ FIRST PRODUCTION

Despite the logical reservations presented, the 'Falco' was immediately welcomed by the Italian pilots. It was endowed with stupendous manoeuvrability, in 1918 it would have wiped out all other aircraft but in 1938 its speed was far inferior to any existing monoplane.

It was therefore decided to mass-produce it in parallel with the new, more modern monoplane fighters (Fiat G.50 and Macchi M.C.200, with which it shared the engine).

Fiat organised its assembly line to the best of its ability to meet the requests received, first and foremost, from the Regia Aeronautica, from Belgium, with 34 aircraft delivered between December 1939 and June 1940, and from Sweden, with 72 aircraft delivered between 1940 and 1941.

Production continued until the end of 1944, eventually numbering no less than 1,820 aircraft built, of which 63 (according to other sources 51) were built under the direct control of the Luftwaffe and 140 completed for export.

Other aircraft were also made for the Hungarian Air Force, which operated with moderate success in the skies over Russia, achieving a positive loss-to-capital ratio.

Still others were given to the Iraqi Air Force. Even Francoist Spain was to some extent invested with some of the new aircraft. These numbers make the 'Falco' the most built Italian aircraft of all time.

In most of the versions built there was no radio equipment.

OPERATIONAL CAMPAIGNS

The new 'Falco' biplane fighter entered service with the Regia Aeronautica in May 1939, being assigned to the 53rd Wing, based at Turin-Caselle. By the outbreak of World War II, some three hundred had already been delivered. On 10 June 1940, the date of Mussolini's declaration of war at Palazzo Venezia, C.R. 42s made up 40 per cent of the entire Italian fighter line. In the course of their military activities, the C.R.42s operated until the armistice for national defence both as day and night fighters. In North Africa, it was also used in a light bomber version (known as an assailant) with two bombs weighing up to 100 kg each placed under the wings (see profile No. 13).

Some examples that survived the conflict were then used in the flight schools of the newly-founded Air Force, including the four groups of the Comando Scuole di Volo based at the Lecce-Galatina airport.

ATTACK ON FRANCE

The first operation involving the C.R.42s in World War II was in June 1944 during the attack on France. Here the "Falco" had their baptism of fire on the morning of 13 June 1940, when twenty-three aircraft of the 23rd Group of the 3rd Wing escorted ten Fiat B.R.20 bombers in an air attack on the French port of Toulon. Twelve fighters strafed the airport of Fayence and Toulon-Hyères Airport, hitting some fifty French planes on the ground, destroying at least twenty.

▲ Fiat C.R.42 of the 162nd Group flying over the Aegean in front of the coast of Anatolia 1940-41. Wikipedia CC 1.0 PD. (See profile 9).

▲ Fiat C.R.42 (stormtrooper version with a load of bombs placed under the wings (in this case the 50kg version) Cyrenaica, Libya 1941.

A few days later, on 15 June, as many as 67 C.R.42s attacked airfields located in southern France. Twenty-seven biplanes of the 150th Group, 53rd Wing, took under their fire the Cuers-Pierrefeu Aerodrome, between the towns of Cuers and Pierrefeu-du-Var, setting fire to some fifteen Vought V-156Fs.

On that occasion, the French air force came to the rescue: seven of the fighters that made cover at 500 m altitude ended up being intercepted by Bloch MB 151s of the AC-3 squadron, which managed to shoot down one C.R.42 and forced another to land.

This second aircraft was then captured intact by the French and immediately re-used in the colours of the transalpine country (see profile 3). The same aircraft, however, was returned to the Italian Air Force the following July after the collapse of the French front.

In the crash, Italian pilots were credited with shooting down four French fighters.

Another 25 C.R.42s headed for Le Luc - Le Cannet Airport, hitting another 20 French aircraft on the ground, destroying some of them. Some French fighters, however, had managed to take off and in the clash they had with the Italians, one 'Falco' and two French aircraft were shot down, while a second Fiat managed to return to the airport although it was badly damaged.

Meanwhile, other transalpine fighters had intercepted the 25 biplanes of the 18th Fighter Group on a covering mission over Beuchamp. In the ensuing combat, the French fighters brought down two C.R.42s. The 18th Group, for its part, claimed the downing of three enemy aircraft, but the *Armée de l'*air (French Air Force) only admitted two losses for the day.

Adjutant Pierre Le Gloan of the GC.III/6 (short for Groupe de chasse III/6 - 'hunting group III/6') on his Dewoitine D.520 managed on the same day to shoot down no less than four C.R.42s and one B.R.20, achieving ace status in a single day.

1 - 1939 FIAT C.R.42 "FALCO" ITALIA

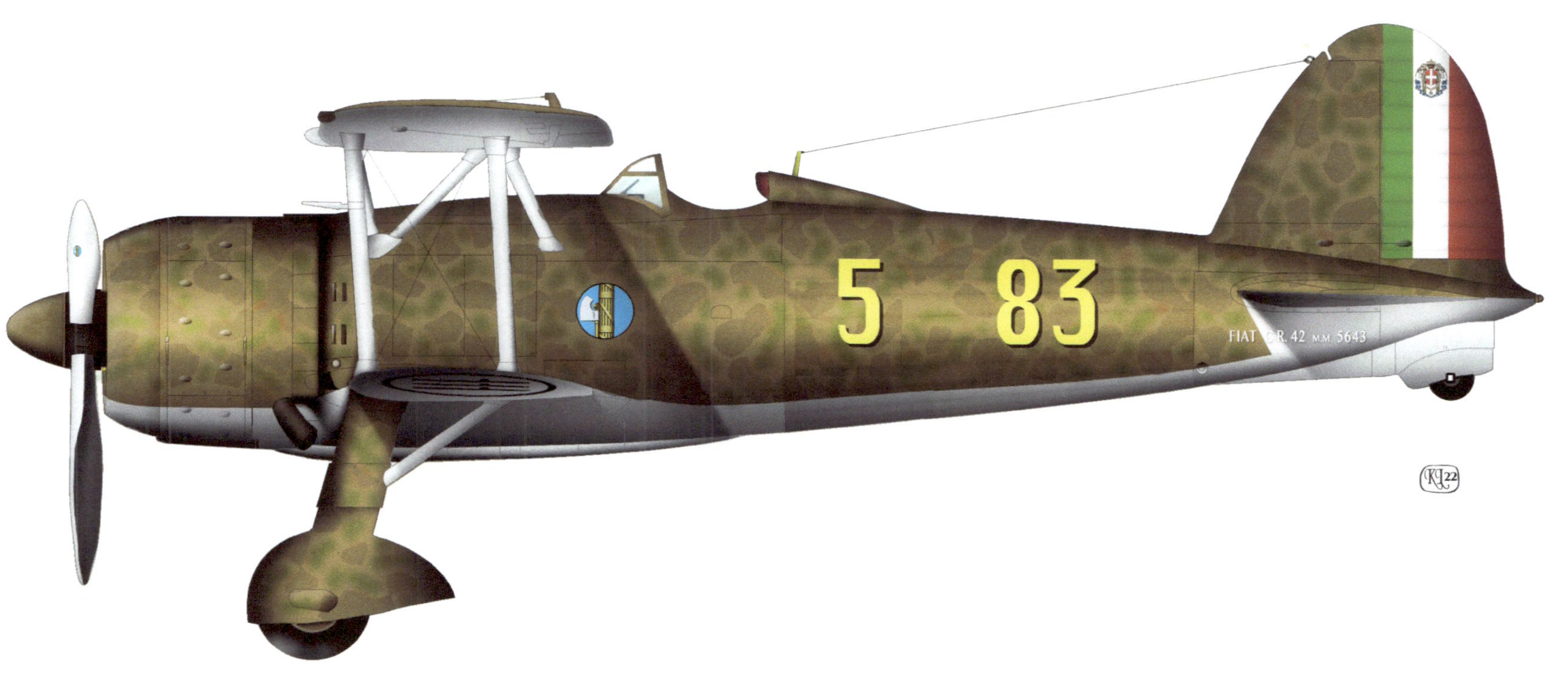

▲ 1939 Fiat C.R.42 "Falco" 5 of the 83rd squadron 18th group Mondovì Italy

▲ 1939-1940 Fiat C.R.42 "Falco" prototype for use as a seaplane

The C.R.42s were then naturally used against the British and consequently also operated on Malta, where they immediately clashed with the Gloster Gladiator, which was outclassed in manoeuvrability by the Italian biplane, and later with the more dangerous Hawker Hurricane. The Fiat, as mentioned, had superior performance to the British biplane. It was much faster at altitudes above 3,000 metres and, thanks to its small wing area, constant-speed propeller and superior engine power, enjoyed great manoeuvrability. The Gladiator, on the other hand, was more manoeuvrable than the Fiat at altitudes below 3,000 m and also had the TR 9 AM radio, while the 'Falco' was without any radio equipment.

Another advantage of the Gladiator was its four Brownings machine guns that fired 2.5 times as many bullets as the Breda-SAFATs mounted on the C.R.42. However, this disadvantage was compensated for by the Italian machine by virtue of its guns of almost double the calibre (12.7mm against the British aircraft's 7.7mm).

This allowed him to hit the Gloster while remaining out of range of the British guns; moreover, the burst of bullets that could hit the British fighter was far more devastating than the one the latter could direct at the C.R.42.

The Breda-SAFATs were, however, very heavy weapons (29 kilograms) but had, as mentioned, a low rate of fire (700 rounds per minute, dropping to 500 when synchronised with a three-blade propeller).

The British machine guns were of an inferior calibre, but thanks to their weight (about 18 kg) they guaranteed 1200 rounds per minute, about 1000 when synchronised. The British also used British incendiary shells, which proved particularly effective, especially when used against low-metal machines such as our C.R.42.

In the operation, on 16 July, British aircraft took off to intercept a dozen C.R.42s of the 23rd Group on a reconnaissance mission over Malta. British officer Keeble machine-gunned a Fiat (probably that of Second Lieutenant Mario Benedetti of the 74th Squadron) but was in turn attacked by Lieutenants Mario Pinna and Oscar Abello.

Keeble engaged in an aerial duel with the two Italian pilots, but his Hurricane was hit in the engine and fell uncontrollably, exploding on the ground near Fort Rinella, followed, a hundred yards away, by Benedetti's Hurricane. Keeble was the first RAF pilot to be killed in action over Malta by C.R.42.

On 31 July, Sergeant Manlio Tarantino's 'Falco' of the 23rd Group shot down one of the three Gloster Gladiators that, according to the legend spread by the British, alone defended the island. The pilot of the Gloster jumped with his parachute, ending up in the sea and suffering severe burns. Meanwhile, another Gloster got the better of him and, after a long manoeuvred fight, shot down the commander of the Italian formation, Captain Antonio Chiodi of the 75th Fighter Squadron, who was decorated with a posthumous gold medal for military valour.

On 24 August 1940, Lieutenant Mario Rigatti of the 75th Squadron, 23rd Autonomous Group CT at the controls of his Fiat C.R.42 "Falco" (M.M.7013) shot down in the skies over Malta the Hawker Hurricane of *Flight Lieutenant* George Burges, of the 261st Squadron, which was attacking a Savoia Marchetti S.M.79. Rigatti, who was also hit, struggled back to Comiso seriously wounded with his badly damaged "Falco" (M.M.7013) and was later awarded a gold medal for military valour.

▲ Side view of the Fiat C.R.42 13 95 participating in the Battle of Britain, on display at the Royal Air Force Museum, London. CC3 Diko (Wikipedia).

▼ Below is another aircraft of the same type (85th Squadron) with slightly different camouflage. CC3 Wikipedia.

FIAT CR 42 "FALCO"

As part of the alliance with Germany, the Fiat C.R.42 sent an air force to northern Europe to fight in the Battle of Britain. Fifty biplanes of the 18th Group, together with forty-five Fiat G.50s, about seventy twin-engine Fiat B.R.20 bombers and some CANT Z.1007 trimotors operated with the Italian Air Corps from bases in Belgium alongside the Luftwaffe against the Royal Air Force in the second half of 1940. On 19 October, the pilots of the C.R.42s all operated at the Ursel airfield, assigned to them as their base. Already the following month, in November, the first battles took place between the Italian biplanes and the Fighter Command's Hurricanes and Spitfires.

On 11 November, forty C.R.42s escorting 10 B.R.20s were intercepted by some thirty Hurricanes of the 46th and 257th Squadrons, together with some Spitfires of the 41st Squadron. In the fierce fighting that followed, the Italian pilots claimed to have definitely shot down nine enemy planes and probably four others, while another British fighter was reportedly shot down by the bombers. However, these victories never found any confirmation in official British documents, according to which the British fighters did not suffer any losses (it was only acknowledged that two Hurricanes were damaged in any case), while the losses admitted by the Italians coincided with those also claimed by the British: two C.R.42s shot down and a third forced to land due to failure on British soil and therefore captured. Signalling the difficulties of these improbable and frankly outnumbered battles, some twenty C.R.42s, which had depleted their fuel reserves during the course of the fight, were forced to make reckless landings on French or Belgian soil during their return to base.

On 23 November, twenty-seven C.R.42s flying offensive reconnaissance between Dunkirk and Calais, clashed with British fighters south-east of Folkestone. The Italian pilots declared that they had engaged some twenty Spitfires in combat, scoring five sure victories and two probable victories, but according to the official British version, the combat was mainly Hurricanes (although there were a few Spitfires), which suffered no losses, while the Italians lost two C.R.42s and a third landed badly damaged and with a wounded pilot on the beach at Calais. In reality, the Italian Air Corps suffered serious losses here, affecting very few.

▲ View of the Fiat C.R.42 forced to land on British soil and captured in perfect working order, undergoing rapid conversion by the RAF for re-use. (Wikipedia).

3 - 1940 FIAT C.R.42 "FALCO" FRANCE

▲ 1940 June Fiat C.R.42 'Falco' captured by the French after a forced landing in Cuer. Returned to the Italian Air Force after the collapse of France at the end of July.

▲ Falco of the 95th squadron, part of the CAI in Belgium, taken in this weird position that has the merit of showing the camouflage used. Wiki.

▼ Belgium 1940, a German Luftwaffe officer sitting in the cockpit examines the control panel of a Fiat C.R.42 56th wing C.T., Italian Air Corp, Battle of Britain. Wikipedia cc1.

▲ Fiat C.R.42 'Falco' 412th Squadron, Barentu, Eritrea 1940 Pilot Captain Mario Visintini Visintini was the first Italian pilot fighter of the Second World War to achieve notoriety as an ace. His exploits in East Africa were all victories at the controls of this manoeuvrable biplane.

5 - 1940 FIAT C.R.42 "FALCO" IN BELGIUM

▲ 1940 Fiat C.R.42 "Falco" Regia Aeronautica, 18th Group, Italian Air Corps in Ursel, Belgium.

The CAI's experience in Belgium, with the 18th Group and its own squadrons - the 83rd, 85th and 95th - which took part in the "Battle of Britain", ended with the meagre results that are known, as often happened before the valour and self-sacrifice of our pilots, who were forced to fight in the harsh northern climate with C. R.'s.R. with open canopies, without any preparation of the machines for the harsh climate in which they were destined to operate, further aggravating the already considerable gap between Spitfire and Hurricane with our biplanes.

■ 1940-41 IN THE GREEK-ALBANIAN SKIES

The Fiat C.R.42 actively participated as an escort fighter and interceptor on the Greek-Albanian front, in the Balkans, the Aegean Sea and the Mediterranean Sea in the last months of 1940 and throughout 1941. Partly due to the fact that it was up against less well-equipped opponents, the Hawk fought well in the Balkan skies, where it most often faced its counterpart, the Gladiator, which the Fiat outclassed in speed and armament. The campaign against Greece was initiated by a few C.R.42s from the 150th Autonomous CT Group (363rd, 364th and 365th Squadrons) and the 160th CT Group (initially with only the 393rd Squadron), based at Coriza.

The "Falco" had their baptism of fire on the same day that the campaign began, 28 October 1940, when they intercepted and attacked a Henschel Hs 126 of the Hellenic Royal Air Force (Ελληνική Βασιλική Αεροπορία), which, however, managed to return to base, despite having 30 bullet holes in its nacelle. Two days later, the C.R.42s achieved their first victories of the campaign when the Fiats of the 393rd Squadron shot down two Henschel Hs 126s of the 3.*Mira*. On 2 November, the "Falco" destroyed two PZL P.24 fighters of the 21.*Mira*. A few days later, a pair of C.R.42s shot down two Greek Breguet Br.19s of the 2.*Mira* and two more Fiats shot down two Vickers Wellingtons of the Royal Air Force - which had begun missions in support of the Greek armed forces - over Vlora.

In order to counter the Italian fighters, which were achieving numerous victories against Greek aircraft and British bombers, the RAF eventually decided to transfer more modern means to Greece. From North Africa came the 80th *Squadron*, led by the great ace Pat 'Marmaduke' Pattle

▲ Several Fiat C.R.42 Falco of the 85th squadron on the runway of Ursel airport in Belgium in the second part of 1940.(Wikipedia).

▲ 1940 Fiat C.R.42 "Falco" Regia Aeronautica, 23rd Squadron of the 70th Group in Sicily, aircraft of Commander Major Tito Falconi.

▲ Summer 1941 Fiat C.R. 42 Falco of the 162ⁿᵈ Group preparing for a flight from Maritza airfield on the island of Rhodes in the Dodecanese. CC3 Wiki.

and staffed by several experienced pilots. After a short period of acclimatisation, the RAF pilots began their containment work by going into action on 19 November 1940, shooting down four Italian fighters in the first aerial combat. This fact began to change the ongoing air battle on the chessboard. Throughout the month of December, the air combat continued furiously with claims of shoot-downs greatly overstated on both sides. In February 1941, the British celebrated their most successful day of air combat in the Greek campaign. In his report on that day, Air Vice-Marshal John D'Albiac, RAF commander in Greece, wrote that the 80th Squadron, re-e-quipped with the Hawker Hurricane, had destroyed, in 90 minutes of aerial combat, as many as twenty-seven Italian aircraft, all victories, the British claim, confirmed and with no losses except the loss of a single Gloster Gladiator. Italian sources, on the other hand, spoke of the loss of only one C.R.42... Even if the number of British victories must be put in perspective, it is undeniable that RAF pilots shot down more aircraft than Italian airmen. There were several reasons for the superiority of the British fighter: at medium-low altitudes, where the fighting took place, the Gladiator was more manoeuvrable than the C.R.42 and the Italian pilots, whose training was centred on aerobatics, were inevitably at a disadvantage in aerial duels. In addition, the enclo-sed cockpit protected the RAF pilots from the harsh conditions of the Greek winter. The radio - which the Fiats lacked - allowed the British pilots to communicate in the air from a distance and thus to adopt more articulate tactics and formations and more effective attack patterns. But the main reason for the superiority of the RAF's fighters was perhaps the human element: while most of the Italian pilots in Greece were aviators just out of flying school, the RAF pilots were more experienced and determined, many were already aces, and above all they were led by one of the RAF's greatest aviators, that 'Marmaduke' Pattle, who had learned to know the weaknes-ses of the Italian fighter and to exploit them to his own advantage.

The C.R.42 was the most modern Italian fighter operating in Italian East Africa (AOI). In the early stages of the war in the Horn of Africa, the 'Falco' fought well against their contemporaries the Gloster Gladiator, Fairey Battle, Vickers Wellesley and Hawker Hart of the South African Air Force. At the outbreak of the conflict, the AOI Air Force Command had 36 C.R.42s distributed between the 412th Squadron in Massawa and the 413th Squadron in Assab. Later, in view of the critical situation, Savoia-Marchetti SM.82 transport planes were set up specifically to carry the dismounted C.R.42s, and in this way 51 new fighters arrived in East Africa to reinforce the air force in that isolated Italian heathland.

On 12 June 1940, AOI's C.R.42s had their baptism of fire when they intercepted nine Vickers Wellesleys of the 47th Squadron in the skies over Asmara. Fighting usually developed when an airport was attacked. Bitter air battles took place in early November during the British offensive against the forts of Gallabat and Metemma along the border with Sudan. The Regia Aeronautica achieved repeated success in these battles, sometimes even against more powerful and armed opponents.

6 November 1940 was perhaps the most successful day of the C.R.42s in the entire Second World War: in a series of fights during the first day of the British offensive against Ethiopia, the Fiat biplanes shot down no fewer than seven Gloster Gladiators, without suffering any losses. In this first phase of the conflict, the figure of Captain Visentini shone above all.

▲ Above: a disassembled C.R.42 inside an SM 82 destined for East Africa. Below: the arrival of a 'Falco' at an AOI airport. CC3 Wiki.

On 29 December, Franco De Michelis and Osvaldo Bartolozzi, of the 413th Squadron, after an aerial duel that lasted about ten minutes, in the Bardery area, managed to shoot down two Hurricanes of No.2 Squadron SAAF. However, already in the remaining 1940s the Italian aircraft began to fall victim to the British wings. Things took a turn for the worse in 1941, when the British forces launched a decisive counter-offensive, the 412th Squadron, tasked with the defence of the Northern Sector, nevertheless became the heroic protagonist of a series of attacks against the British, again led by the legendary figure of Mario Visentini. Thus on 9 February, at dawn, five C.R.42s from the 412th Squadron, led by Mario Visintini, succeeded in destroying or disabling no less than 16 enemy aircraft. Unfortunately, shortly afterwards Visentini himself died in a similar operation. On 6 June 1941, only two C.R.42s remained operational in East Africa. Pilot Malavolta's last Italian Fiat fell on 24 October and was the last air combat in East Africa. Here Italy lost a total of some 90 Falco.

NORTH AFRICA

At the beginning of the conflict in Libya, there were 127 C.R.42s divided between the 13th Fighter Group (2nd Wing) at Castel Benito, 10th Group and 9th Fighter Group (4th Wing) at Benina, including reserve aircraft. And it was on the African fronts that the Italian machine achieved its best successes.
In this chessboard, 'thermal' issues were of little consequence, and here the Italian pilots were almost all veterans of the Spanish Civil War. It was precisely a pilot who had become an ace in Spain, Captain Franco Lucchini, who first shot down an RAF aircraft during the desert war, four days after Italy's entry into the war; it was a Gladiator, which was also the RAF's first loss in the desert. In June, the reported culls already amounted to fifteen: 11 Bristol Blenheim, 3 Gladiator and one Short Sunderland.
Soon, however, the Allies' technical differential led the Regia Aeronautica to suffer real defeats. Thus, in the following July, the Italian Air Force lost no less than twenty Falco.

▲ The Fiat C.R.42 belonging to the 73rd Squadron, part of the 4th Wing, piloted by Ernesto Botto, nicknamed "Iron Leg"; North Africa 1940. CC3 Wiki.

▲ 1940 Fiat C.R.42 "Falco" Regia Aeronautica, MM4393 of Major Ernesto Botto commander of the 9th Group, 4th Wing in Benina (Libya).

▲ Fiat C.R.42 CN night fighter version in its typical black livery and fitted with an elongated flame-proof exhaust system. 1942.

With more modern, single-winged aircraft, several RAF pilots soon became 'aces' of their own against the Italians in North Africa, such as the South African Marmaduke 'Pat' Pattle, one of the greatest Allied aces. The problem was also aggravated by the fact that even the Gladiators, on paper inferior to the Falco, had indisputable advantages; in particular, this was due to the presence of the radio, which could allow coordinated attacks, crucial for gaining the initial advantage of surprise, but also an overall superiority of the British aircraft in low-altitude performance. In this context, life for the Italian air force in North Africa proved increasingly difficult. In December, many Gladiators switched over to Hawker Hurricanes and life became increasingly difficult for our biplane. Nevertheless, thanks to the skill of the pilots and its manoeuvrability, the C.R.42 was partly able to cope successfully with faster and more armed monoplanes.

This unexpected resistance from the Falco and their experienced pilots forced those of the Hurricanes to adopt the tactics that the Messerschmitt Bf 109 pilots employed against them - avoiding melee (in which the C.R.42s displayed their acrobatics) and attacking with sudden dive-bombing. Despite the 'hit-and-run' tactics adopted by the British, our aircraft continued to enjoy successes, such as on 14 April 1941 at Tobruk or in November 1941, when Captain Bernardino Serafini, commander of the 366th Squadron, shot down a Hurricane, and again on 10 July 1942, when a 'Hawk' even claimed the downing of a Spitfire.

But these were the last successes of the Italian biplane: in April 1941, supplanted by the Macchi M.C.200 'Saetta' in the role of pure interceptor, with the delivery of the first 14 C.R.42 Wing Bombs, the C.R.42 was used almost exclusively as a light bomber, revealing an unhoped-for validity, thanks to the robustness of its structure and the radial engine's resistance to ground strikes. On 19 June 1942, the last 82 surviving C.R.42s left Africa and returned to Italy.

The C.R.42s were practically the only night fighters of the Regia Aeronautica, even though they continued to lack radar and often even radio transmitters. This choice was made to compensate for the technical deficiencies that Italian biplanes encountered during the course of the war against more modern aces. The first nighttime shoot-down by an Italian pilot in World War II was carried out by Captain Giorgio Graffer, commander of the 365th Squadron, 150th Group, 53rd Wing. On the night of 13-14 August 1940, Graffer fired on the Whitley Mk.V bomber, which was flying to bomb the Fiat in Turin. When his machine guns jammed, Graffer did not hesitate to ram the bomber before parachuting out. The Whitley attempted to return but ended up crashing into the English Channel. On 12 July 1941 a Wellington was probably shot down near Benghazi by a Fiat of the 18th Group. On 5 December of the same year, a C.R.42CN of the 356th Squadron definitely shot down another bomber of the same type near Naples.

The night of 25 August 1942 was perhaps the most successful for the Italian night fighter. Lieutenant Colonel Armando François, commander of the 4th Wing, took off in a C.R.42, intercepted and shot down an unidentified twin-engine bomber that fell into the sea 4 km from the coast. After landing, Lieutenant Giulio Reiner boarded the same plane and, guided by radio, intercepted a Wellington of the 70th Squadron. Reiner hit the bomber's bomb bay, which crashed 10 km southeast of Fuka, exploding.

There are reports from other units of certain or probable shoot-downs of four other twin-engine bombers (also Wellington and Bristol Blenheim). The C.R.42CNs still operational shortly before the armistice achieved the greatest successes. On the night of 22-23 February 1943, Lieutenant Luigi Torchio of the 377th Autonomous Squadron scored the first of his five victories during the conflict, shooting down a Wellington in the skies over Palermo with a C.R.42.

▲ Fiat C.R. 42- CN "Falco" of the 167th Group, 300th Squadron No. 7 preparing to take part in a night fighter operation taking off from Boccadifalco airfield near Palermo. February 1942. State Archives.

▲ 1940 Fiat C.R.42 "Falco" 97 MM5021, of the 4th Wing 9th Group 97th Squadron - in Libya.

VERSION OF THE VEHICLE

■ **FIAT C.R.42 MAIN VERSIONS**

C.R.42AS

'Tropicalised' version to operate in North Africa. It was equipped with a sand filter on the carburettor intake, extended radiator, larger propeller spinner. There were the C.R.42AS/CB or C.R.42AS/BA sub-variants with the introduction of bomb racks, up to a maximum weight of 100 kilos, at the strong point of the wing struts.

C.R.42 CAI (BELGIUM)

Aeroplanes destined for the CAI (Italian Air Corps) were equipped with an armoured seat (already adopted as standard during the Series I), an 80-litre auxiliary tank in the fuselage, replacement of a 12.7 mm machine gun with a 7.7 mm gun (to save weight), virosbandometer, improved oxygen system and rocket launcher gun; only one aircraft had an IMCA ARC transceiver radio. 1 I in the UHF band (see profile 5).

C.R.42 CN

They were the famous night fighter 'Falco'. Equipped with a two-way radio, with extended exhausts, sometimes extending beyond the cabin to hide the detector flares, interceptor beacons, augmented instrumentation and, sometimes, illuminating bombs. To compensate for the increase in weight, one or both guns were replaced with 7.7 mm. In the beginning, the aircraft were painted matt black, with energy boosters (see profile14).

C.R.42EC

EC stands for Chemical Dispenser, supplied with two smoke screen generators under the wings.

C.R.42 Aegean

Produced in a few dozen units, this set-up featured the same 80-litre fuel tank already adopted in Belgium, which increased its autonomy.

C.R.42 ICR

The hydro version was studied as early as 1938 by Fiat, which then entrusted its construction to CMASA in Marina di Pisa. The only prototype was built in 1940. At the beginning of the following year, testing began at Vigna di Valle on Lake Bracciano. The ICR reached 423 km/h, the range went up to 950 km, and the tangency went down to 9,000 metres. Empty weight rose from 1 720 to 1 850 kg, total weight from 2 295 to 2 425 kg. Not being preferable to the IMAM Ro.43 and IMAM Ro.44 already underway, it was never produced (see profile 2).

C.R.42RF

Photographic Recogniser: at least six examples were built equipped with an Rb camera. 50.

C.R.42R

(Tug) for towing gliders.

C.R.42LW

Night attack version intended for the Luftwaffe.

C.R.42B

It was the two-seater version, the most modified, with an elongated fuselage and tandem second seat, intended for training. About forty examples were made, modifying existing airframes from Agusta and Caproni Trento. Length increased by 68 centimetres to 8.94 metres. The height decreased by 23 centimetres while the empty weight increased by only 40 kilos to 1,760 kilos, thanks to the removal of the wheel and wheel fairings. The total weight rose to 2,300 kilos. Top speed was 430 km/h at 5,300 metres. Until 1945, the two guns were retained.

C.R.42DB

Built in March 1941, this example (MM.469) was an attempt to revitalise the project by installing the engine yoke of a Macchi C.202 on a production C.R.42, with a German Daimler-Benz DB 601 engine. Flown by test pilot Valentino Cus, the prototype recorded speeds well in excess of 500 km/h and was the subject of an order for 150 examples, which was soon cancelled.

■ C.R.42 SWEDES

The Swedes adopted for several of their Falco the addition of special skids in place of wheels in order to be able to take off and land on snowy spaces. In addition, the Swedish Falco were fitted with the Bristol Mercury VIII engine (manufactured under licence by NoHAB).

▲ C.R.42 in an airfield in January 1941. Greek Albanian front. Courtesy State Archives.

▲ A Fiat C.R.42 set on fire on the ground by an enemy air attack in Tobruk. PD courtesy by Australian War Memorial.

▼ Fiat C.R.42 formerly operated in the Aegean during the war and now preserved or the Air Force Historical Museum in Vigna di Valle. Wiki CC3 by Zerosei.

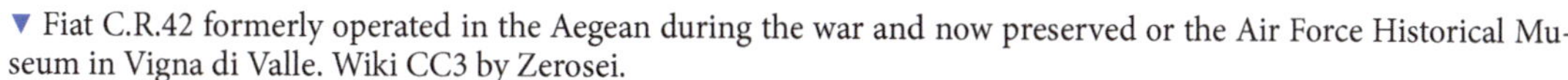

▲ 1941 May Fiat C.R.42 bis "Falco" 10, 75th Squadron, 23rd C.T. Group, 1° Stormo C.T. Regia Aeronautica Comiso, Sicily.

10 - 1941 FIAT C.R.42 "FALCO" IN RHODES

▲ 1941 Fiat C.R.42 "Falco" 161st Squadron, 161st Autonomous Group C.T. Maritsa (Rhodes Dodecanese).

▲ Fiat C.R. 42- CN "Falco"of the 167th Group, 300th Boccadifalco Airport Squadron 1942. State Archives.

11 – 1942 FIAT C.R.42 "FALCO" RAVENNA (ITALY)

▲ 1942 April Fiat C.R.42 b.a. nr. 45 MM.6682 of the Ravenna Assault Fighter School, with ring-pattern camouflage typical of Aermacchi fighters.

12 - 1942 FIAT C.R.42 "FALCO" TUNES

▲ 1942 August Fiat C.R. 42 'Falco' of the 387th squadron (Puss in Boots).

13 - 1942 FIAT C.R.42 "FALCO" CIRENAICA

▲ 1942 October Fiat C.R.42 AS 'Falco' of the 15th Assault Wing, in Cyrenaica (Libya). Pilot Colonel Raffaele Colacicchi, during his career he achieved the world record for endurance in inverted flight in 1933.

▲ 1942 Fiat C.R.42 AS "Falco" C.N. 6 of the 377th Autonomous Squadron Palermo-Boccadifalco. Fighter piloted by Captain Luciano Marcolin. Painted completely black for the night hunt to which the fighter was assigned in the second part of the conflict

▲ 1940 some Fiat-CR-42-Falco-18. JG56 of the 3rd Wing, 18th Group, 85th Squadron at Ursel airfield in Belgium during CAI operations for the Battle of Britain. Wikipedia

▼ Fiat C.R.42 in 1940 in Belgium. 'Falco' of the Eighty-third Squadron, 18th C.T. Group. Pinterest

15 - 1942 FIAT C.R.42 "FALCO" HUNTING SCHOOL FOLIGNO (ITALY)

▲ 1942 Fiat C.R.42 FOL-4 Foligno Hunting School Italy.

16 - 1942 FIAT C.R.42 CN "FALCO" CIAMPINO (ITALY)

▲ 1942 Fiat C.R.42 of the 300th squadron, Autonomous Group C.N. Ciampino Airport.

▲ 1942 Fiat CR.42 b.a. nr. 45 MM.6682 of the Ravenna Assault Fighter School, with ring-pattern camouflage typical of Aermacchi fighters. See Profile 11. Wikipedia

▼ Fiat C.R.42 catturato dagli inglesi dopo la ritirata italiana dall'Africa Settentrionale nel 1943. Image IWM PD

▲ Fiat C.R.42 of the 82nd Squadron of the 13th Group 2nd Wing. C. T., operated at the Gambut military airfield located in Cyrenaica in September 1940. CC3 Wiki by Martin Čížek

                    FIAT CR 42 "FALCO"

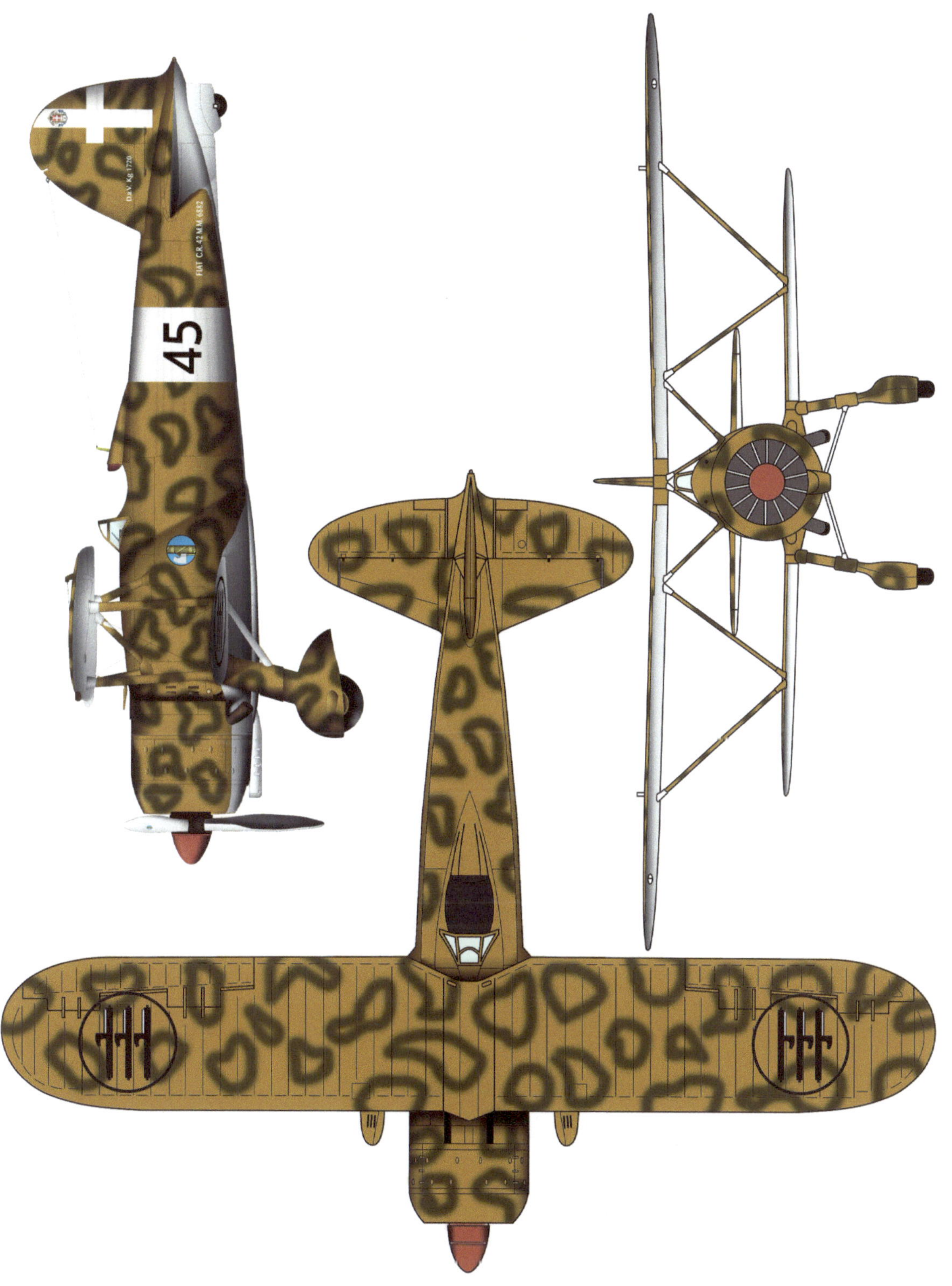

▲ 17 - 1943 Fiat C.R. 42 full profile

▲ A Fiat C.R.42 CR.42 light bomber type in Sicily 1943. Photo Aviazione Militare Italiana, F.Anselmino.

▲ Fiat C.R.42 in 1941 in Rhodes at the military airport of Maritza and belonging to the 161st-162nd Group. CC3 Wiki.

18 - 1940 FIAT C.R.42 "FALCO" BELGIUM

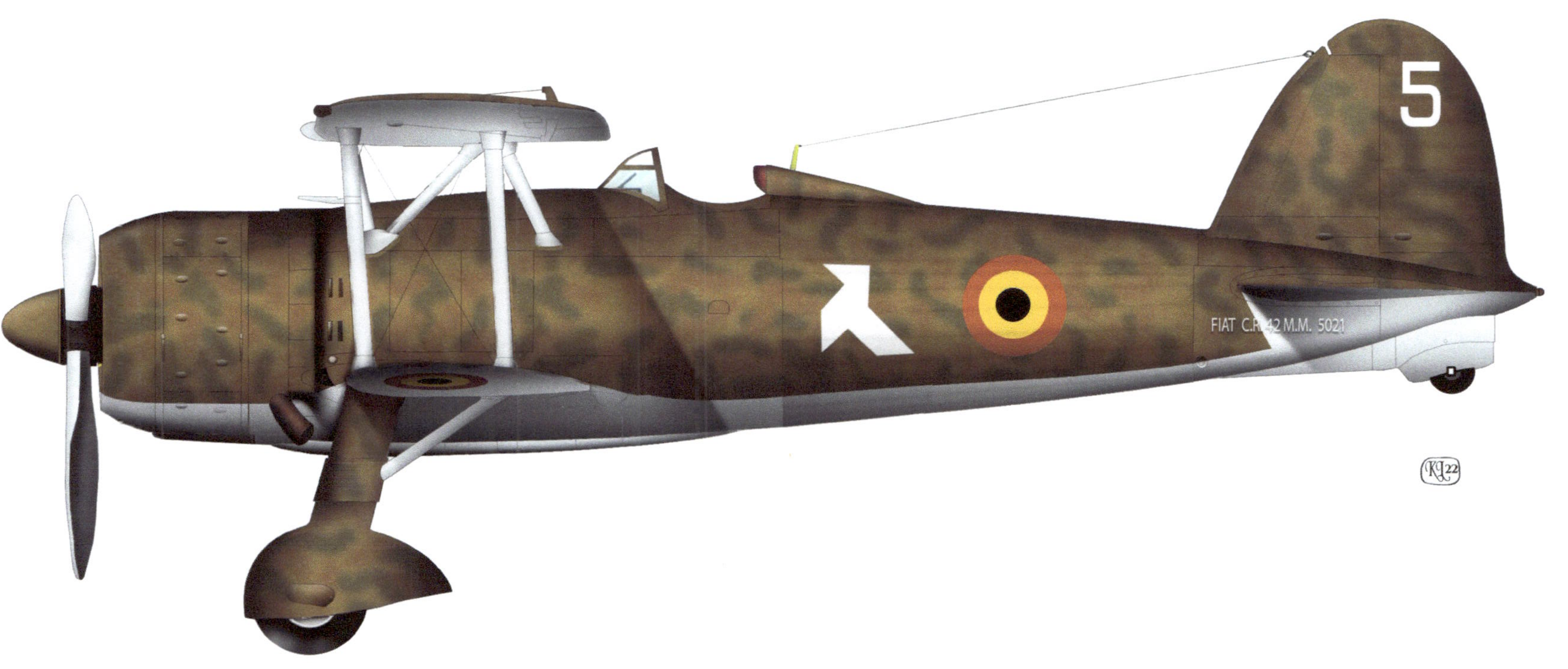

▲ 1940 Fiat C.R. 42 5 of the 4th Squadron, 2nd Fighter Group Belgian Air Force in Nivelles (Belgium).

▲ Fiat C.R.42 already operational in the Aegean campaign. Detail of the frame and wing suoport. Wiki CC3 by Zerosei.

▼ Fiat C.R.42 and Fiat G50 destroyed on the ground at an airfield near Tripoli in Libya in 1943. Australian Archives PD.

19 - 1941 FIAT C.R.42 "FALCO" HUNGARY

▲ 1941 Fiat C.R. 42 of the 1/3rd Ricsi Fighter Squadron of the Hungarian Air Force in Russia.

▲ Fiat CR. 42 of the 1/3rd Ricsi Fighter Squadron of the Hungarian Air Force in Russia. See Profile 20. Wikipedia

▼ Another image of the Fiat C.R.42 captured by the British because it was forced to land during the Battle of Britain in 1940. Wiki CC3.

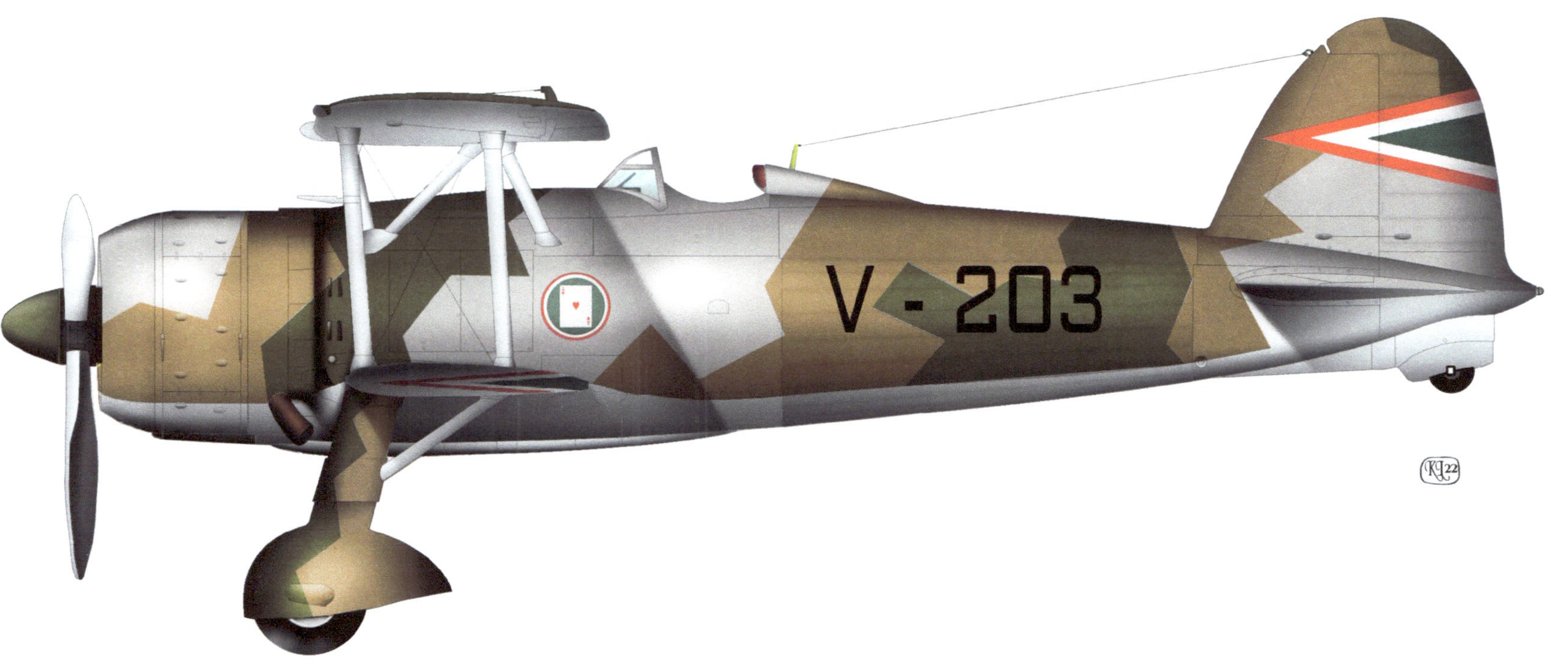

▲ 1941 Fiat C.R. 42 of the 2/3rd Squadron of the Hungarian Air Force (ace of hearts).

▲ 1941 Fiat C.R.42 Swedish No. 11. Belongs to Svenska Flygvapnet 11th Squadron based in Sweden.

EXPORT OF THE AIRCRAFT

In addition to the Italian Air Force, which was obviously the largest user of the aircraft, several nations took an interest in this versatile aircraft. Among the Allied forces, the C.R.42 mainly equipped the Hungarian Air Force and to a lesser extent the Croatian Air Force. Germany was also a major user of the aircraft both before and after the armistice.

The aircraft, however, inherited a good reputation and was sold to several other nations before the war. Among them, the most interesting orders were from Belgium, Sweden and Iraq.

A few were lost or captured by Axis enemies, such as Great Britain, France and South Africa.

■ MAIN USER COUNTRIES

BELGIUM: Belgium's Aviation militaire was among the first to take an interest in the Italian biplane project. Belgium received an initial batch of 39 C.R.42s, serial number NC.221-269. The order started in November 1939. The onset and subsequent outbreak of the conflict curbed this delivery to some extent. It is estimated that around 30 aircraft were actually delivered. They were immediately used to counter the German attack where they apparently performed quite well.

HUNGARY (Magyar Királyi Honvéd Légierő): the Magyar country was already an old customer of Fiat having purchased C.R.32s in the past. The Hungarian air force ordered the first new Italian biplanes as early as 1938. The supply for Hungary was divided into three lots of, respectively, 18 (NC. 300-317), 32 (NC.318-349) and 18 aircraft (NC.401-418). The Hungarian Falco were renamed V.2. These aircraft were used first against Yugoslavia and then more heavily against the Soviet Union where they had the best win/loss rating ever achieved by C.R.42.

CROATIA (Zrakoplovstvo Nezavisne Države Hrvatske): ordered an unknown number of C.R.42 aircraft.

GERMANY: the Luftwaffe placed an order for 63 Fiat in 1943-44 (XV series), Werk-Nr. 10001-10063. The armistice of 8 September did not stop production of the obsolete biplane, which the Germans usually used in police operations in the Balkans. The Fiat C.R.42LW (LW stands for Luftwaffe) was produced until the violent bombing raids of April 1944 severely damaged the Italian assembly lines. It was a German C.R.42 that shot down a P38 in February 1945, it was the last downing by a biplane in history.

SWEDEN (Svenska Flygvapnet): at first it was Finland that ordered 12 'Falco' (lot NC.2501-2512) but the Finnish Air Force later rejected them outright; they were thus taken over by the Swedish Air Force to equip Säve's Flottilj F-9. The order placed by Sweden later increased to 60 C.R. 42s (CN. 2523-2572).

IRAQ: Royal Iraqi Air Force: the exact number of this order is unknown.

SOUTH AFRICA: Suid-Afrikaanse Lugmag: operated with a few captured ex-Air Force aircraft mainly in Africa.

GREAT BRITAIN: the British captured an early C.R.42 which was forced to land on British soil in 1940. Repaired and reactivated, it began operating under the new British insignia. Subsequently, the British captured many more in Africa.

▲ Two of the best-known prototypes of the C.R. 42. Above, the Fiat C.R.42 DB being run-in. Its Daimler-Benz DB 601 engine made it the fastest biplane ever built. The C.R.42 DB, which had the experimental serial number MM 469 and was quickly built, flew for the first time in March 1941, and testing was entrusted to Commander Valentino Cus, the same man who had flown the prototype of the normal 42. The Ministry of Aeronautics considered the creation of a two-seater for fast reconnaissance, but this solution was also abandoned and the C.R.42 DB was not developed.

▼ Fiat C.R. 42 ICR The hydro version was studied as early as 1938 by Fiat, which then entrusted its construction to CMASA of Marina di Pisa. The only prototype was built in 1940. At the beginning of the following year, testing began at Vigna di Valle on Lake Bracciano. The ICR reached 423 km/h, the range went up to 950 km, and the tangency went down to 9,000 metres. Empty weight rose from 1 720 to 1 850 kg, total weight from 2 295 to 2 425 kg. As it was not preferable to the already launched IMAM Ro.43 and IMAM Ro.44, it was never produced.

▲ A Hungarian Air Force Fiat C.R. 42 (Magyar Királyi Honvéd Légierő. CC3 WIKI by Fortepa

▼ Fiat C.R.42 of the Belgian Air Force on the runway of the Nivelles airfield. CC3 WIKI.

22 - 1942 FIAT C.R.42 "FALCO" SWEDEN

▲ 1942 Fiat C.R.42 Swedish. Belongs to Svenska Flygvapnet from the Kiruna base in Sweden. Winter version with skids for take-off in the snow.

▲ 1942 Fiat C.R. 42 of the 5/1st Hungarian squadron used for night hunting.

24 - 1942 FIAT C.R.42 CN "FALCO" GERMANY

▲ 1943 Fiat C.R. 42 AS serving in the Luftwaffe 20 Nachtschlactgeschwader (NSG) in Strasbourg, France.

DATA SHEET

FIAT C.R. 42 "FALCO"	
Parameter	**Data**
Crew	1
Length	8,26 m
Wingspan	9,70 m (superior) and 6,50 m (inferior)
Height	3,30 m
Wing surface area	22,4 m²
Empty weight	1.720 kg (excluding armament)
Max take-off weight	2.295 Kg
Wing loading	102 kg/mq
Fuel capacity	420 liters
Engine	Fiat A. 74 RC. 38
Power	840 CV (618 kW) at 3,800 metres
PERFORMANCE	
Maximum speed	430 km/h at an altitude of 6,000 m
Climbing speed	approx. 12 metres per second
Take-off run	210 m
Landing	340 m braking
Autonomy	775 km (1,000 km the Aegean and CAI versions in Belgium)
Tangency	10.500 m
Minimum speed	128 km/h at low altitude
ARMAMENT	
Armament	Two 12.7 mm Breda-SAFAT machine guns Or 2 x 7.7 mm Or 1 x 12.7 mm and 1 x 7.7 mm 2 x 50 kg bombs Or 2 x 100 kg bombs (C.R.42 AS)

WW2 ITALIAN TANK AIRCRAFT COLORS & CAMOUFLAGE

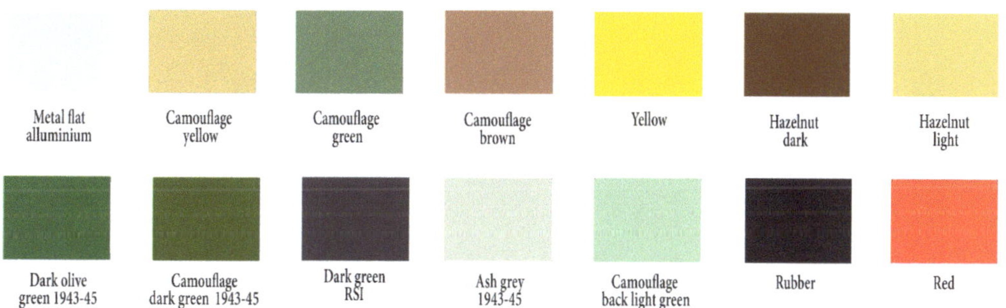

Metal flat alluminium	Camouflage yellow	Camouflage green	Camouflage brown	Yellow	Hazelnut dark	Hazelnut light
Dark olive green 1943-45	Camouflage dark green 1943-45	Dark green RSI	Ash grey 1943-45	Camouflage back light green	Rubber	Red

▲ Swedish Air Force Fiat C.R.42 (J-11) stored at the Flygvapenmuseum in Linköping, with typical Scandinavian country insignia. CC3 WIKI by Alan Wilson.

▼ Another Swedish Falco, this time equipped with skids for landing and take-off on snow slopes. Wikipedia.

BIBLIOGRAPHY

- Apostolo, Giorgio. Fiat C.R. 42, Ali e Colori 1 (in Italian/English). Torino, Italy: La Bancarella Aeronautica, 1999. No ISBN.
- Apostolo, Giorgio. Fiat C.R. 42, Ali d'Italia 1 (in Italian/English). Torino, Italy: La Bancarella Aeronautica, 1998. No ISBN.
- AA.VV. Caccia Assalto - Dimensione Cielo. Edizioni Bizzarri, Roma 1973
- Avions militaires 1919–1939 – Profils et Histoire (in French). Paris: Hachette, Connaissance de l'histoire, 1979.
- Bernàd, Denes, Dmitriy Karlenko and Jean-Lous Roba. From Barbarossa to Odessa – The Luftwaffe and Axis Allies strike South-East: June–October 1941 – Volume 1 Hinckley, Ian Allan Publishing, 2007. ISBN 978-1-85780-273-3.
- Beale, Nick, Ferdinando D'Amico and Gabriele Valentini. War Italy: 1944–45. Shrewsbury, UK: Airlife Publishing, 1996. ISBN 1-85310-252-0.
- Boyne, Walter J. Scontro di Ali (in Italian). Milano: Mursia, 1997. ISBN 88-425-2256-2.
- Carr, John, On Spartan Wings, Barnsley, SY: Pens & Sword Military, 2012. ISBN 978-1-84884-798-9.
- Cattaneo, Gianni. The Fiat C.R.42 (Aircraft in Profile no. 170). Leatherhead, Surrey, UK: Profile Publications Ltd., 1967. No ISBN.
- Cull, Brian and Frederick Galea. Gladiators over Malta: The Story of Faith, Hope and Charity. Malta: Wise Owl Publication, 2008. ISBN 978-99932-92-78-4.
- De Marchi, Italo. Fiat C.R.42 Falco (in Italian). Modena, Italy: Stem Mucchi, 1994. No ISBN.
- Domange, Yves (March 1999). "Quand les démocraties occidentales achetaient des avions dans l'Italie fasciste… (2ème partie: la Belgique et l'Angleterre)" [When Western Democracies Bought Their Aircraft from Fascist Italy… (Part 2: Belgium and England)]. Avions: Toute l'aéronautique et son histoire (in French) (72): 40–47. ISSN 1243-8650.
- Forslund, Mikael. J 11, Fiat C.R. 42 (in Swedish with English summary). Falun, Sweden: Mikael Forslund Production, 2001. ISBN 91-631-1669-3.
- Garello, Giancarlo (May 2001). "La chasse de nuit italienne (1ère partie: les débuts)" [Italian Night Fighters: The Beginning]. Avions: Toute l'Aéronautique et son histoire (in French) (98): 10–13. ISSN 1243-8650.
- Garello, Giancarlo (June 2001). "La chasse de nuit italienne (1ère partie: les débuts)" [Italian Night Fighters: The Beginning]. Avions: Toute l'Aéronautique et son histoire (in French) (99): 19–24. ISSN 1243-8650.
- Green, William and Swanborough, Gordon. "Fighter Biplane Finale…The Falco". Air Enthusiast, No. 20, December 1982–March 1983. pp. 1–14. ISSN 0143-5450.
- Gustavsson, Håkan and Ludovico Slongo. Fiat C.R.42 Aces of World War 2. Midland House, West Way, Botley, Oxford /New York, Osprey Publishing, 2009. ISBN 978-1-84603-427-5.
- Gustavsson, Håkan and Ludovico Slongo. GLADIATOR vs. C.R.42 FALCO 1940–41. Midland House, West Way, Botley, Oxford /New York, Osprey Publishing, 2012. ISBN 978-1-84908-708-7.
- Gustavsson, Håkan. "South African Air Force use of the Fiat C.R.32 and C.R.42 during the Second World War." Håkans aviation page, 9 April 2009. Retrieved: 13 April 2009.
- Haining, Peter. The Chianti Raiders: The Extraordinary Story Of The Italian Air Force in The Battle Of Britain. London: Robson Books, 2005. ISBN 1-86105-829-2.
- Kopenhagen, W. Das große Flugzeug-Typenbuch (in German). Stuttgart, Germany: Transpress, 1987. ISBN 3-344-00162-0.
- Lambert, John W. "The 14th Fighter Group in World War II". Atglen, Pennsylvania: Schiffer Military History, 2008. ISBN 0-76432-921-9.
- Lucas, Laddie, ed. Wings of War: Airmen of All Nations Tell their Stories 1939–1945. London: Hutchinson, 1983. ISBN 0-09-154280-4.

- Massimello, Giovanni and Giorgio Apostolo. Italian Aces of World War 2. Oxford / New York: Osprey Publishing, 2000. ISBN 978-1-84176-078-0.
- Neulen, Hans Werner. In the skies of Europe – Air Forces allied to the Luftwaffe 1939–1945. Ramsbury, Marlborough, UK: The Crowood Press, 2000. ISBN 1-86126-799-1.
- Pacco, John. "Fiat C.R.42" Belgisch Leger/Armee Belge: Het militair Vliegwezen/l'Aeronautique militaire 1930–1940 (in French). Artselaar, Belgium, 2003, pp. 66–69. ISBN 90-801136-6-2.
- Pagani, Flaminio. Ali d'aquila Duelli Aerei nei Cieli d'Europa 1936–1943 (in Italian). Milano: Mursia, 2007.
- Punka, George. Fiat C.R. 32/C.R. 42 in Action (Aircraft Number 172). Carrollton, Texas: Squadron/Signal, 2000. ISBN 0-89747-411-2.
- "S.C." (in Italian). Il Messaggero Roma, 12 July 1984.
- Sgarlato, Nico. Fiat C.R.42 (in Italian). Parma, Italy: Delta Editrice, 2005.
- Skulski, Przemysław. Fiat C.R.42 Falco. Redbourn, UK: Mushroom Model Publications, 2007. ISBN 83-89450-34-8.
- Sutherland, Jon and Diane Canwell. Air War East Africa 1940–41 The RAF versus the Italian Air Force. Barnsley, South Yorkshire, UK: Pen and Sword Aviation, 2009. ISBN 978-1-84415-816-4.
- Taghon, Peter (December 1998). "Les FIAT C.R.-42 de l'Aéronautique militaire belge (1)" [The FIAT C.R.-42s of the Belgian Air Force]. Avions: Toute l'aéronautique et son histoire (in French) (69): 2–11. ISSN 1243-8650.
- Taghon, Peter (January 1999). "Les FIAT C.R.-42 de l'Aéronautique militaire belge (fin)" [The FIAT C.R.-42s of the Belgian Air Force]. Avions: Toute l'aéronautique et son histoire (in French) (70): 12–17. ISSN 1243-8650.
- Taylor, John W.R. "Fiat C.R.42." Combat Aircraft of the World from 1909 to the present. New York: G.P. Putnam's Sons, 1969. ISBN 0-425-03633-2.
- Thomas, Andrew. Gloster Gladiator Aces. Botley, UK: Osprey Publishing, 2002. ISBN 1-84176-289-X.
- Vossilla, Maggiore. "Pilota Ferruccio, comandante 18° Gruppo C.A.I (in Italian)." Prima Battaglia Aerea Relazione giornaliera Ministero dell'Aeronautica, 11 Novembre 1940.
- Wheeler, Barry C. The Hamlyn Guide to Military Aircraft Markings. London: Chancellor Press, 1992. ISBN 1-85152-582-3.
- Winchester, Jim. "Fiat C.R.42." Aircraft of World War II (The Aviation Factfile). Kent, UK: Grange Books plc, 2004. ISBN 1-84013-639-1.
- Rivistea JP4 - Mensile di Aeronautica, 6, anno XXXIV, giugno 2005.
- Rivista Aeronautica, maggio 1997, giugno 2001, marzo 2005.

▲ Fiat C.R.42 preserved by USAF - National Museum of the U.S. Air Force PD

BOOKS ALREADY PUBLISHED

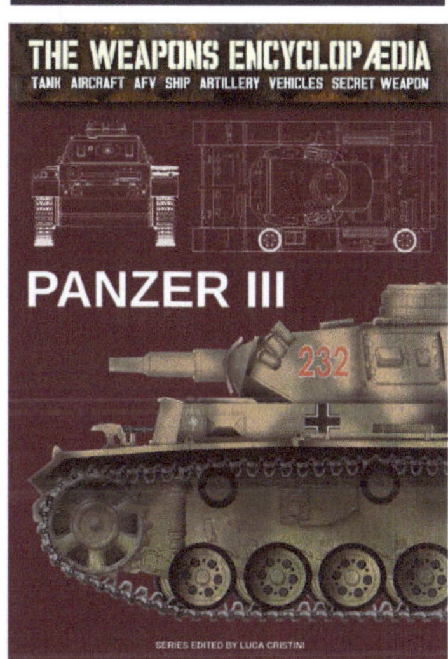

TWE-009 EN

www.ingramcontent.com/pod-product-compliance
Lightning Source LLC
LaVergne TN
LVHW071620180726
843512LV00002B/210